PIANO SOLO

NOMADLAND

MUSIC FROM THE MOTION PICTURE SOUNDTRACK

The following songs are the property of:
Bourne Co.
Music Publishers
www.bournemusic.com
ANSWER ME, MY LOVE

ISBN 978-1-7051-5130-3

Visit Hal Leonard Online at
www.halleonard.com

Contact us:
Hal Leonard
7777 West Bluemound Road
Milwaukee, WI 53213
Email: info@halleonard.com

In Europe, contact:
Hal Leonard Europe Limited
42 Wigmore Street
Marylebone, London, W1U 2RN
Email: info@halleonardeurope.com

In Australia, contact:
Hal Leonard Australia Pty. Ltd.
4 Lentara Court
Cheltenham, Victoria, 3192 Australia
Email: info@halleonard.com.au

CONTENTS

OLTREMARE

By LUDOVICO EINAUDI

GOLDEN BUTTERFLIES

from SEVEN DAYS WALKING: DAY 1

By LUDOVICO EINAUDI

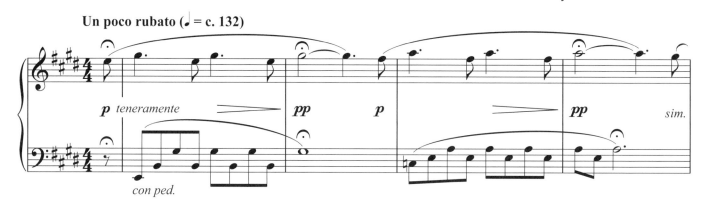

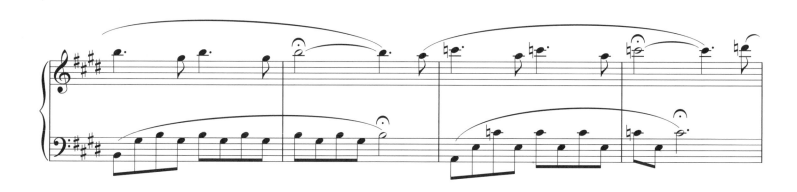

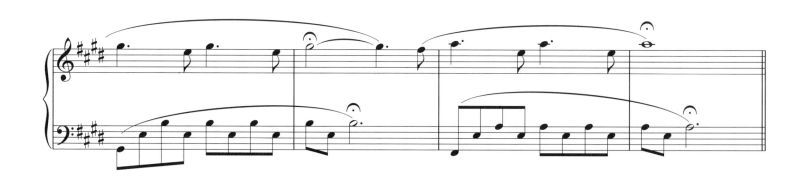

Fluente, senza rubato (♩ = c. 132)

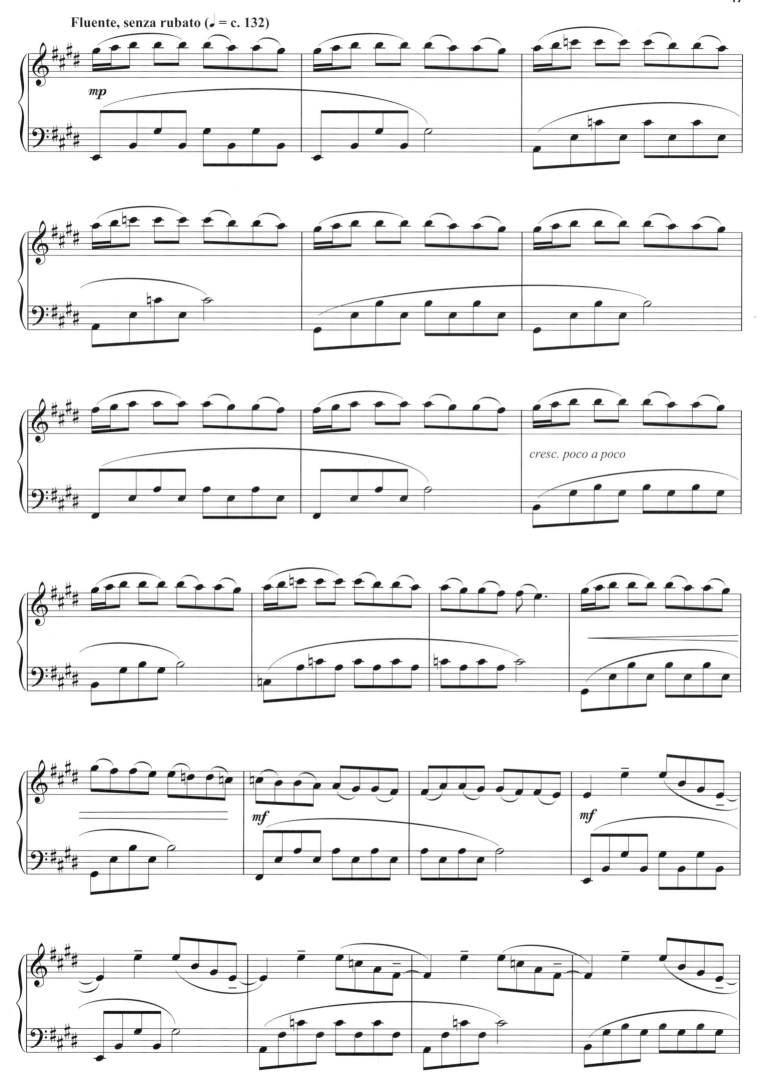

Calmo, un poco rubato (♩. = c. 118)

Grandioso, senza rubato

EPILOGUE

By ÓLAFUR ARNALDS

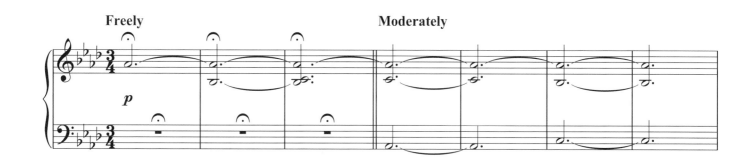

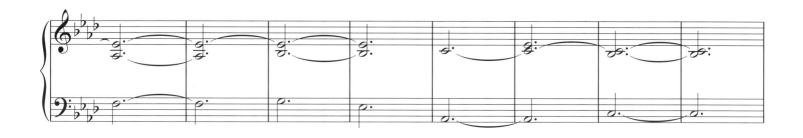

ANSWER ME, MY LOVE

Words and Music by GERHARD WINKLER
and FRED RAUCH
English Lyric by CARL SIGMAN

Lyrics:

An - swer me, oh my love, just what sin have I been guil - ty of? Tell me how I came to lose your love? Please an - swer me, my love. You were mine

DAVE'S SONG

By TAY STRATHAIRN

Slowly, in 2

Pedal ad lib. throughout

* Duet "four hands" arranged for piano soloist.

PETRICOR

By LUDOVICO EINAUDI

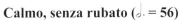

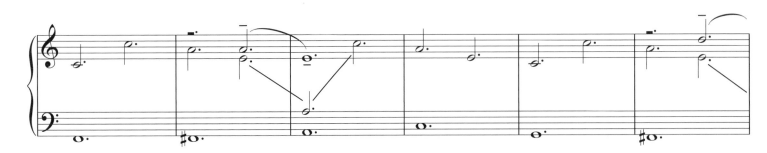

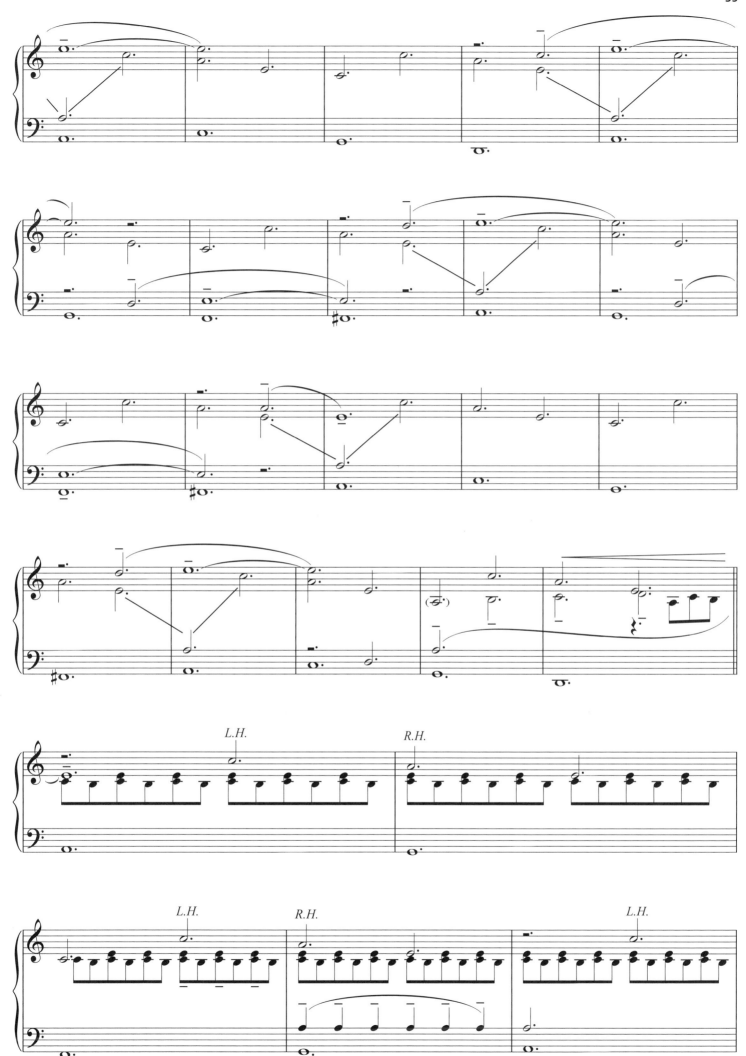

Con brio, l'istesso tempo

Calmo, l'istesso tempo

Con brio, l'istesso tempo

Calmo, l'istesso tempo

LOW MIST

from SEVEN DAYS WALKING: DAY 1

Music by LUDOVICO EINAUDI

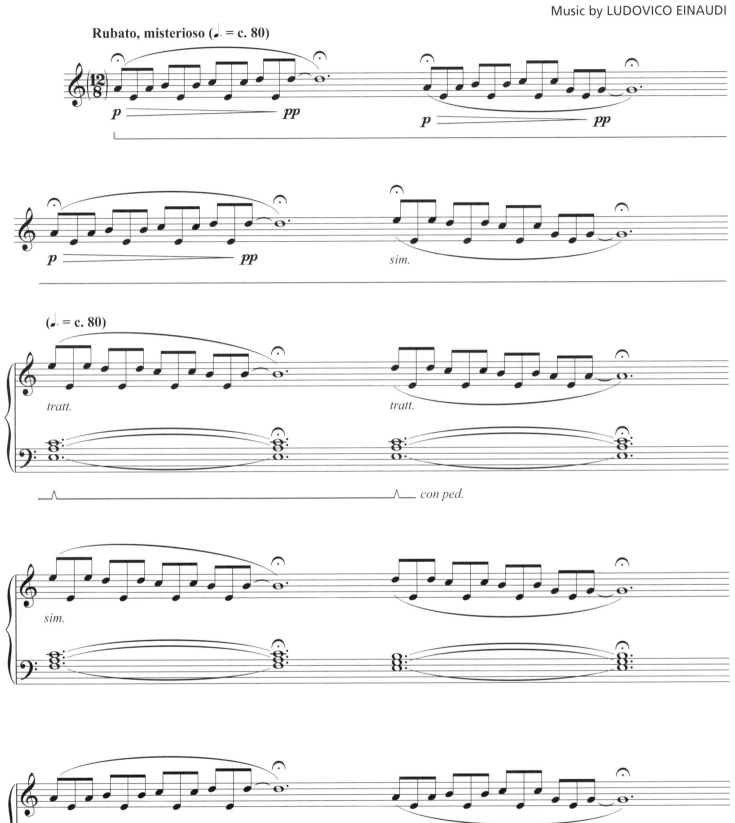

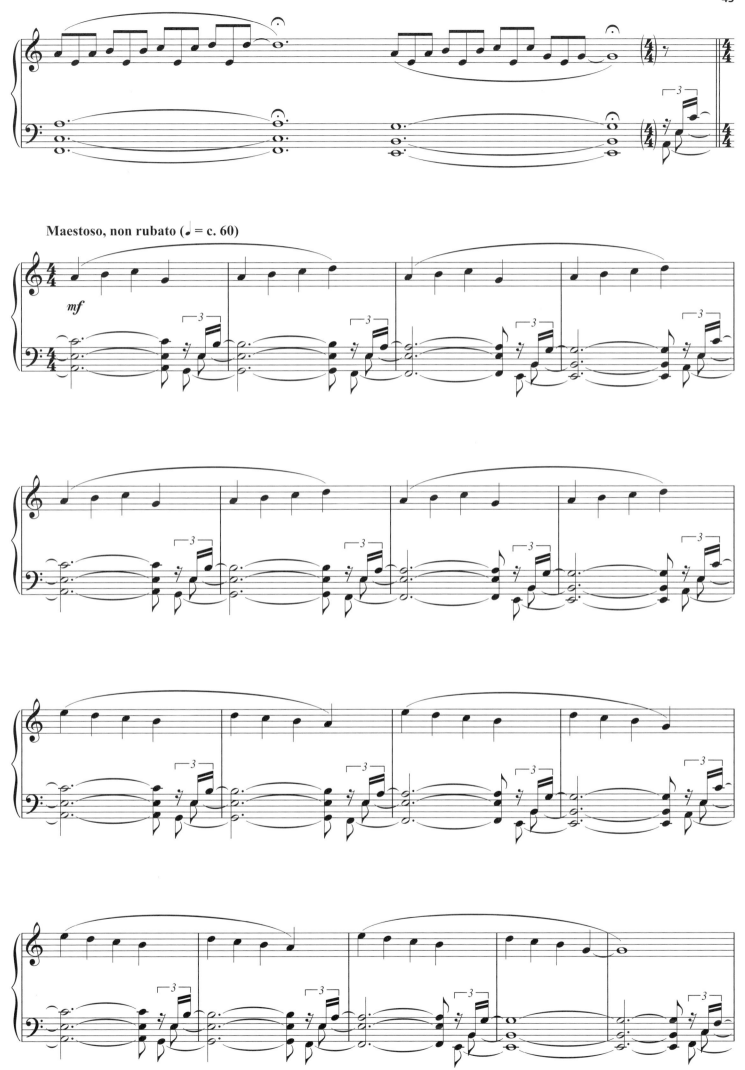

Un poco più mosso (♩ = c. 66)

mf *deciso*

espressivo